Peter Stadelm

Setting Up
An Aquarium

CONTENTS

T Y P I C A L
AQUARIUM FISH

- Attractive and brightly colored

- Quiet housemates

- Interesting to watch

- Easy to care for

- A source of tranquility

- Ideal pets for those allergic to animal hair

- No problems during vacation

An aquarium makes a splendid attraction in your home. In addition, it always offers something interesting to observe: how a male Swordtail, by swimming rapidly forward and backward, tries to win the favor of his female; how a female Molly gives birth to live young, or how various species care for their broods or construct bubble nests. Have fun!

TO HELP YOU DECIDE

1 The aquarium needs a site where it can remain permanently.

2 The site should also allow side access for maintenance.

3 The nearby wall should contain a grounded outlet. When using extension cords, the dangerous possibility exists that water will drip into the outlet and cause a short circuit.

4 An aquarium must be cared for regularly. When performing maintenance tasks, try not to rush. Postponing maintenance when you do not have enough time will be better for the fish in the long run.

5 An aquarium is an oasis of calm in the hustle and bustle of everyday life.

6 Allergy sufferers will have very few problems with an aquarium.

7 The routine expenses for food and electricity are extremely low.

8 Bear in mind: A 24-inch (60-cm) long aquarium weighs 130 pounds (60 kg). Your aquarium will be safe only on a base that is specifically built to hold it.

The Aquarium as Room Divider

Do you want to place your aquarium against a wall, as is usually done, or have you already considered using it as an attractive room divider? An aquarium over 30 inches (80 cm) long can be set up nicely in this capacity. Placing one narrow side against a wall and having views from both sides require special decoration. It is like a cross section of a stream whose banks slope up gently to the left and right. The swimming area is open in the middle, larger plants stand at the sides, and rocks and roots prevent the terraces from slipping down toward the middle. Remember, the deepest part lies in the center and should not be obstructed by decorative elements.

CHOOSING AND BUYING THE FISH

Fish display a wide range of bright colors and interesting behaviors. So many fascinating species exist that the aquarium hobbyist must find out as much as possible about the requirements of the fish before buying and then choose accordingly.

Choosing the Right Fish

The wider the selection of fish, the harder the choice. However, you should learn as much as possible before buying so that you group only fish that get along well together and whose requirements are compatible. Even if a large number of fish species appeal to you, you should make a selection and not overstock your aquarium. Fish that do not have enough room to live are susceptible to disease.

The species on pages 10 to 21 will help you choose your fish. You must also know the Latin names of the species you have chosen; this is the only way to avoid mix-ups. In the trade, very different names are often used for the same fish. If you ask the salesperson for a fish by using its Latin name, you are certain to get the right fish.

Tip: First buy the aquarium with the necessary equipment, the decorations, and the plants. After at least three days, put in the algae eaters, and do not feed them for eight days. Add the remaining fish gradually (see pages 22–23). These stocking suggestions have proven very successful.

Male Dwarf Gourami captivate with their bright colors.

Where to Get Fish

In my experience, friends can be a good source for young fish (fry) when they are looking to change their fish communities. Getting fish from friends is a great idea, but only if their aquariums are clean and well cared for, and the water conditions match that of your aquarium. Fish have little tolerance for changes in water quality.

Most likely, however, you'll be making a trip to the pet shop. Your local pet store offers a large selection of healthy fish all year long, and trained personnel can give advice and assistance for all types of aquariums.

Keep in mind that for a new aquarium you should buy the fish in several consecutive lots. After the break-in period (3 to 10 days, depending on the size of the tank), algae eaters like Flying Foxes or Bristle-nosed Catfish are added first as the cleanup detail. The remaining fish are best introduced in two groups 10 to 14 days apart.

Tip: Careful aquarists keep newly purchased fish in quarantine for about four weeks. The quarantine tank must be equipped just as completely as the community tank. However, it should not contain any other fish.

Checklist
Buying Fish

1 The aquarium dealer's tank should be planted, have clear water, and have clean glass. There should be no dead fish in the tank.

2 Feel free to buy young fish even if they are less colorful and smaller than adults.

3 Avoid the busiest hours at the store so that the salesperson is not rushed. The fish are also less stressed then.

4 It's important to know that tiny white spots or white cottonlike growths, dull skin, and frayed fins are unmistakable indications of disease.

5 Observe the behavior of the fish. Healthy fish swim around in a lively way and are not timid.

6 Observe how the fish eat. Healthy fish eat rapidly.

7 Buy food the fish are accustomed to eating at the same time you buy the fish.

Transporting the Fish

The pet dealer packages the fish in a plastic bag half filled with water. A layer of newspaper is wrapped around it for insulation. Now you should go home as quickly as possible. Transporting the animals puts them under great stress. The shorter you make the trip, the better. Be sure to keep the bag horizontal while carrying it so the fish have more room to swim. Besides, more oxygen gets into the water through the greater water surface.

Adding Fish to the Tank

Fish are cold-blooded animals whose body temperature conforms to the outside temperature. They cannot tolerate sudden changes in temperature.

Therefore, do not put the fish into the tank right away. Instead, first float the unopened bag on the water. Now wait a while until the water temperature in the transport bag and that of the aquarium have equalized. After about 15 minutes, put the water conditioner with protective slime coating additive into the aquarium, open the bag, and slowly mix the water in the bag with the aquarium water. Pour in aquarium water with a cup until the bag is full. Then tip the bag, and let the fish swim out.

Species of Aquarium Fish

On the following pages, you will find a selection of easy to care for fish that are best kept at a water temperature of 75 to 79°F (24 to 26°C) and a pH of 6.5 to 7.5. The sizes given are based on experience with aquarium fish. In the wild, their sizes can differ.

Live-bearing Tooth Carps
Family Poeciliidae

In the male live-bearing tooth carps, the anal fin has been transformed into a reproductive

Harlequin Rasboras (**Rasbora
heteromorpha**) *are happiest in a school.*

organ, the gonopodium. During mating, this is
inserted into the female's vent and transfers a
packet of sperm. These fertilize the eggs that
have developed in the female, and some are
stored. The dark spot indicates the presence of
fertilized eggs. The eggs develop within the
mother's body until they hatch and reach the
water as fully developed fry.

Care: Keep these fish in a tank at least 24
inches (60 cm) long with good plant growth
and a dense layer of floating plants on the surface. pH must be above 7. Spawning traps,
available in pet stores, keep the fry from being
eaten. The mother is fished out after she has
given birth, and the fry are safe from predators.

Food: Feed flake food and mosquito larvae
(frozen). The fry need finely powdered food.

Guppy (*Poecilia reticulata,* see photos pages
13 and 24). Males grow to 1.2 to 1.6 inches (3 to
4 cm), females grow up to 2.3 inches (6 cm).
Many strains are larger. This is a lively swimmer
that appreciates small groups (four to six members of the same species). If possible, keep more
females than males. Guppies are susceptible to
fin rot and fungal infection, so do not keep them
together with typical fin-nippers like Tiger Barbs.

Swordtail (*Xiphophorus helleri,* see photos
pages 46, 58). These are 1.9 to 2.7 inches (5 to
7 cm) long. Males are lively and spirited. They
like to display constantly in front of each other
and harass their females intensely. Therefore in
a 40-inch (1-m) tank, keep two males with four
to six females. These are useful algae eaters.

PORTRAITS:
AQUARIUM FISH

Aquarium fish are remarkable for their wide variety of forms, which fascinate every observer. The attractive fins of the Fighting Fish or the enormous caudal fins of the Guppies are exciting examples.

Photo above: Brilliantly colored male Siamese Fighting Fish (Betta splendens).

Photo above: Zebra Danio (Brachydanio rerio).

Photo right: Bleeding Heart Tetra (Hyphessobrycon erythrostigma).

Photo above: Male Dwarf Gourami (Colisa lalia). In this species, the pectoral fins have been transformed into threadlike tactile orga

Photo below: Red-eye Tetra
(Moenkhausia sanctaefilomenae).

*Photo above: Red
Platy* **(Xiphophorus
maculatus).**

*Photo right:
Female Guppy*
(Poecilia reticulata).

*Photo above:
Flying Fox*
**(Epalzeorhynchus
kallopterus).**

*Photo right:
Tiger Barbs*
(Puntius tetrazona)
*are robust
schooling fish.*

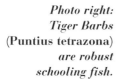

Photo above: Pearl Gourami
(Trichogaster leeri).

Platy (*Xiphophorus maculatus*, see photos pages 13 and 16). Males are 0.8 to 1.2 inches (2 to 3 cm) long, and females grow to 1.2 to 1.6 inches (3 to 4 cm). These lively fish live in small groups (five to seven fish) and graze on algae.

Similar to care for: The related Variable Platy (*Xiphophorus variatus*, see photo, page 61) yields interesting color strains when hybridized.

Black Molly (*Poecilia sphenops*, see photo page 18). These lively fish grow to 1.6 to 2.3 inches (4 to 6 cm) in length and are happy living in a small group (four to six members of the same species). They scour the aquarium for algae, and are prolific breeders. They are sensitive to very soft water and pH values below 7.

Labyrinth Fish
Suborder Anabantoidei

These colorful fish owe their name to a specialized organ in the rear part of the head, the labyrinth organ. With its help, the fish, who generally live in oxygen-poor water, can also take in atmospheric oxygen. In the Gourami, the pelvic fins have been transformed into filaments and serve as tactile organs. Their reproduction is remarkable. The males of most species build very compact bubble nests at the surface of the water. To do this, they take air bubbles from the water surface, coat them in their mouths with a sticky mucous secretion, and finally blow them out at the water surface. A fortress of bubbles is soon built up. The eggs are then placed there and cared for by the male until they hatch. These fish are best kept as pairs.

Care: Care is possible in tanks at least 24 inches (60 cm) long and better in tanks over 30 inches (80 cm) long. Use dense planting around the outside edges with a partial covering of floating plants.

Avoid strong currents. Labyrinth Fish, except for the Paradise Fish (*Macropodus opercularis*), prefer warm water. Therefore, 77°F (25°C) is the minimum temperature.

Food: Use dried food and frozen live food for variety.

Dwarf Gourami (*Colisa lalia*, see photos pages 8, 12, 56). This placid, 1.6-inch long (4-cm) long fish usually stays in the upper level of the tank. Keep only with small schooling fish or bottom-dwelling fish that do not nip at the long, threadlike pelvic fins. Males are brilliantly colored, females are paler.

Plants like the Red Amazon Swordplant offer good hiding places.

Similar to care for: The beautiful Honey Gourami (*Colisa chuna*), 0.8 to 1.2 inches (2 to 3 cm) long, is similar. Do not keep these together with very lively fish. Blue Gourami (*Trichogaster trichopterus,* see photo page 18) grow up to 4 inches (10 cm) long and are a very robust species. The tank must be at least 30 inches (80 cm) long. Pearl Gourami (*Trichogaster leeri,* see photos pages 13 and 56), 4 inches (10 cm) long, should not be kept together with lively fish like Tiger Barbs.

Paradise Fish (*Macropodus opercularis,* see photo page 54). Males are brilliantly colored and have a longer caudal fin than the plumper female. The most robust Labyrinthfish is 2.3 to 3.1 inches (6 to 8 cm) long. Place one pair into a 30-inch (80-cm) tank. These will often annoy slow-moving ornamental fish.

Siamese Fighting Fish (*Betta splendens,* see photos pages 12, 57). These grow up to 2.7 inches (7 cm) long. Only the males are aggressive among themselves and toward other long-finned tank mates. One male and several females can be kept in a community tank.

Barbs, Danios, and Rasboras
Order Cypriniformes

Barbs owe their name to the short barbels (Latin: *barba* = beard) that have developed in many species to the left and right of the mouth, and often on the lips as well, as tactile organs. With their brilliant coloring and their lively nature, they brighten up a community tank marvelously. Smaller species should not be kept together with the more robust larger species, otherwise the smaller ones will pine away.

Care: Keep in tanks at least 24 inches (60 cm) long. Include plantings around the edges, create partial shading by floating plants. Leave plenty of free swimming space. A darker bottom and roots accentuate the beauty of these fish. They are sensitive to pH values over 7.5; a pH of 6.5 would be ideal.

TIP

Solicitous Parents

The female Golden-eyed Dwarf Cichlid (*Nannocara anomala*) displays incredible solicitude for her brood. This normally peaceful fish is positively belligerent when defending her young. Sometimes the female even tries to include thawing frozen food, which is slowly sinking to the bottom of the tank, in the school of fry and protect it as well.

Food: Use all the usual types of food (see page 45).

Harlequin Rasbora (*Rasbora heteromorpha,* see photo page 11). These schooling fish grow 1 inch (2.5 cm) long and look best in a group of at least seven to ten animals. These lively, peaceful fish should not be kept together with rough, larger schooling fish. pH must not be above 7.

Tiger Barb (*Puntius tetrazona,* see photos pages 13, 28). These grow to 1.6 inches (4 cm) long. They are schooling fish, with the largest male setting the tone in a group of five to seven animals. They are lively and robust and should not be kept with slow-moving and long-finned fish. They like to nip.

Zebra Danio (*Brachydanio rerio,* see photo page 12). These 1-inch (3-cm) long, active schooling fish are happiest in a larger group (seven to eight fish). They like to stay just below the surface of the water and are ideal for keeping with all fish except placid fish. This species also spawns in the community tank. As long as a carpet of floating plants covers a small part of the water surface, some fry will survive. They can hide there when pursued by other tank mates.

Half-striped Barb (*Puntius semifasciolatus var.*, see photo page 40). These grow to 2 inches (5 cm) in length and are lively schooling fish that should be kept in small groups (four to six animals). They are constantly on the move in search of food and eat brush algae!

Flying Fox (*Epalzeorhynchus kallopterus,* see photo page 13). They are one of the most important algae eaters, grow 2.7 to 3.9 inches (7 to 10 cm) long, and are undemanding and gregarious. Although often somewhat aggressive among themselves, they need hiding places for periods of rest.

Wagtail Platy (**Xiphophorus maculatus**) *pluck algae from decorations and plants.*

Catfish
Order Siluriformes

Catfish are indigenous throughout the world. In the aquarium, catfish are useful as scavengers since—depending on the species—they clean up algae and leftover food.

Care: Place them into tanks over 24 inches (60 cm) long. Shade with floating plants. Provide shelters with roots and rock caves and free space near the tank bottom.

Food: They eat all the usual types of food (see page 45).

Bronze Corydoras (*Corydoras aeneus,* see photo page 64). These are 2-inch (5-cm) long bottom dwellers that enjoy moving around in a group (three to five fish) and scour the bottom of the tank for food. Use tablets for specific feeding.

Upside-down Catfish (*Synodontis nigriventris,* see photos pages 2, 19). These grow to 2.7 inches (7 cm). In tanks over 30 inches (80 cm) long have three to five animals. They need several shelters but usually all congregate in one. This species often swims on its back.

Bushy-mouthed Catfish (*Ancistrus species aff. dolichopterus,* see photo page 19). The male is about 4.7 inches (12 cm) long, and the female is a bit smaller (other *Ancistrus* species grow to about 8 inches [20 cm] long). This species is the most effective algae eater in the aquarium and is solitary. It needs it own cave, which it will defend against intruders, but it's very peaceful outside the cave. The males develop an impressive headdress of branched antennae.

Similar to care for: All Loach species.

Cichlids

Family Cichlidae

Cichlids are territorial, form stable pairs in many species, and regularly spawn in the community tank. The fry are defended against potential enemies. The species presented here remain so shy that they can be kept in community tanks without problem.

Care: Keep them in tanks over 24 inches (60 cm) long. Some of the young can be raised in the community tank if

Bristle-nosed Catfish like to have a cave where they can hide.

microscopic food (in small quantities) is squirted directly into the school of fry with a thin PVC tube.

Food: They eat a varied diet (see page 45).

Kribensis (*Pelvicachromis pulcher,* see photos pages 4 and 18). Males grow up to 3.9 inches (10 cm) long. Females (red blotch on each flank) grow considerably smaller. Keep one pair in a tank 30 inches (80 cm) long. This species needs a cave as the center of its territory. Even if only one pair is kept, two caves should be a good distance apart so that the female has a place to retreat.

Cockatoo Dwarf Cichlid (*Apistogramma cacatuoides,* see photos pages 18, 36, 38). Males grow to 2.3 to 3.1 inches (6 to 8 cm), females are up to 2 inches (5 cm) long. One male is always kept with several females (two in a 24-inch [60-cm] tank, three in a 30-inch [80-cm] tank). Each animal needs it own cave, which must be sufficiently far away from the others.

Golden-eyed Dwarf Cichlid (*Nannacara anomala,* see photo page 19). Females have a checkerboard pattern, males are blue and usually twice as large as the approximately 2-inch (5-cm) long female. They are peaceful outside of the spawning period. After spawning, the females are pugnacious since they are anxious about the fry.

Ram (*Papiliochromis ramirezi*). These grow up to 2-inch (5-cm) long and are the most peaceful Cichlid. Rams form stable pairs and occupy a small territory. It is especially delightful to keep two pairs in a sufficiently large tank (at least 24 inches [60 cm] long); they will frequently display before each other along their territorial boundaries.

PORTRAITS:
AQUARIUM FISH

Aquarium fish come in all hues and colors. They provide a true feast for the eyes with their iridescent tones, for example the Rainbowfish.

Photo above: The colors of the Cockatoo Dwarf Cichlid (Apistogramma cacatuoides) *are captivating.*

Photo belo *Blue Goura* (Trichogast trichopteru

Photo above: Red Phantom Tetra (Megalamphodus sweglesi).

Photo below: Kribensis (Pelvicachromis pulcher), *female left.*

Photo above: Black Mollies (Poecilia sphenops) *are very lively fish.*

Photo below: Female Golden-eyed Dwarf Cichlid (Nannacara anomala).

Photo above:
Neon Tetra
(Paracheirodon
innesi).

Photo right: Boeseman's
Rainbowfish
(Melanotaenia
boesemani).

Photo below: Male Bushy-mouthed Catfish (Ancistrus species aff. dolichopterus) *with numerous antennae.*

Photo above: Two Upside-down Catfish (Synodontis nigriventris).

Angelfish (*Pterophyllum scalare*, see photo, page 56). These grow up to 5.9 inches (15 cm) long and 7.8 inches (20 cm) deep. They need a tank at least 30 inches (80 cm) long with a minimum depth of 20 inches (50 cm). The most important decorative elements are long, tall structures, like the leaves of the Amazon Swordplant. The Angelfish float quietly among the plants at lookout posts. They live in groups, with the individual animals staying a slight distance away from each other. They are placid fish that do not tolerate lively company. These are best kept in a small group of four to six animals in a 40-inch (1-m) tank stocked with other placid fish, for example Neon Tetras, Congo Tetras, Black Mollies. Do not keep Angelfish with fin-nippers.

Characins
Order Characiformes

Characins are schooling fish that, in the wild, move through

Juvenile Rams (Papiliochromis ramirezi).

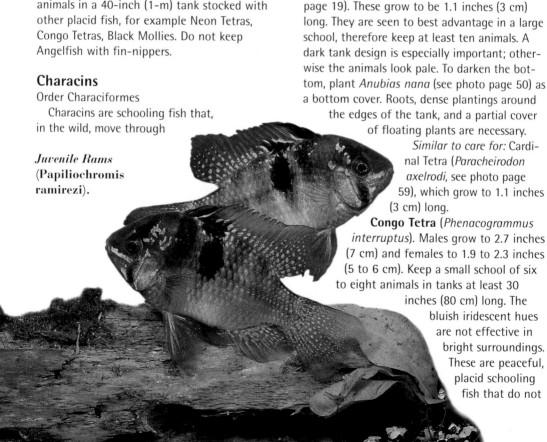

the water in mixed or separate schools. They are agile and often very colorful. They pine away without the company of others of their species. A characteristic of this family of fish is the adipose fin, a small fin at the base of the tail.

Care: Keep them in tanks at least 24 inches (60 cm) long. Dense planting around the edges and partial shading by floating plants are necessary.

Food: Use dried food supplemented with mosquito larvae, or use freeze-dried or frozen food supplemented with vitamins.

Neon Tetra (*Paracheirodon innesi*, see photo page 19). These grow to be 1.1 inches (3 cm) long. They are seen to best advantage in a large school, therefore keep at least ten animals. A dark tank design is especially important; otherwise the animals look pale. To darken the bottom, plant *Anubias nana* (see photo page 50) as a bottom cover. Roots, dense plantings around the edges of the tank, and a partial cover of floating plants are necessary.

Similar to care for: Cardinal Tetra (*Paracheirodon axelrodi*, see photo page 59), which grow to 1.1 inches (3 cm) long.

Congo Tetra (*Phenacogrammus interruptus*). Males grow to 2.7 inches (7 cm) and females to 1.9 to 2.3 inches (5 to 6 cm). Keep a small school of six to eight animals in tanks at least 30 inches (80 cm) long. The bluish iridescent hues are not effective in bright surroundings. These are peaceful, placid schooling fish that do not like overactive company. Males have elongated dorsal, caudal, and anal fins with lustrous white edges. They are best not kept together with fin-nippers (but this species is quick and can defend itself).

Black Tetra (*Gymnocorymbus ternetzi*). These schooling fish 0.8 to 1.6 inches (2 to 4 cm) long occupy the middle level of the tank. The rounded shape of the body and black coloring make a lovely contrast with slender, colorful animals like Neon Tetras.

Similar to care for: Red-eye Tetra (*Moenkhausia sanctaefilomenae*, see photos pages 13, 27) are similar. They grow to 2 inches (5 cm) long and occupy the upper level of the tank.

Rosy Tetra (*Hyphessobrycon bentosi*, see photo page 29). These are 1.6 inches (4 cm) long and need the company of other members of their species. However, they do not swim constantly in a school. The more attractive males display before each other with outspread fins and briefly occupy small courtship territories.

Similar to care for: Phantom Tetras (*Megalamphodus*), which are 0.8 inches (2 cm) long, Emperor Tetra (*Nematobrycon palmeri*, see photo page 51), which are 1.2 inches (3 cm) long, and Black Neon Tetra (*Hyphessobrycon herbertaxelrodi*), which are 1.6 inches (4 cm) long, are similar. Another similar species is the Bleeding Heart Tetra (*Hyphessobrycon erythrostigma*, see photos pages 12, 41), which are 2.3 inches (6 cm) long, need a tank at least 30 inches (80 cm) long, and go together especially well with Congo Tetras.

Rainbowfish

Family Melanotaeniidae

In the morning hours, these fish glow with the most intense colors because this is the time

T I P

Fish as Weather Forecasters

Have you ever wondered why your fish seem especially colorful some days? They are giving you an indication of a pending change in the weather.

When a storm front or some other strong change in the atmospheric pressure is on the way, the Ruby Barbs suddenly appear particularly brightly colored, and the dorsal fins of Congo Tetras turn pale pink. The fish are beginning to court or are spawning. Watch for it sometime!

when courtship and spawning take place. The colors look especially intense if a little daylight is entering from the side.

Care: Use tanks at least 30 to 40 inches (80 to 100 cm) long, include dense plantings, and provide plenty of free swimming space. They are sensitive to pH values below 7.

Food: They eat all the usual types of food (see page 45).

Boeseman's Rainbowfish (*Melanotaenia boesemani*, see photo page 19). Males grow up to 3.9 inches (10 cm), and females are up to 3.1 inches (8 cm) long. These lively schooling fish (keep five to seven fish) are most active in the morning. They spawn readily on Java Moss. A dark tank background accentuates the golden orange color.

Similar to care for: Most other *Melanotaenia* species are similar. A well-known one is the Banded Rainbowfish (*Melanotaenia trifasciata*, see photo page 6), 4.7 inches (12 cm) long.

Selecting the Right Fish for a Community

You cannot just put fish together in a tank without using some thought. Rowdy, playful fin-nippers and peaceful occupants are not compatible. Furthermore, water quality and temperature requirements must be well matched. In the following table, you will find sample fish communities. If you put together your fish community yourself, pay attention to the following:

✔ Many fish have preferred habitats: some like to remain near the water surface, others in the middle level, many near the bottom. Find out about the habits of the fish and choose so that every level is occupied.

✔ Take with a grain of salt the rule of 0.5 inches (1 cm) of fish length per 1.5 to 2 quarts (1.5 to 2 liters) of water. For example, 30 Cardinal Tetras require as much room as one pair of Kribensis. The amount of fecal material produced, and thus the waste disposal problem, is likewise identical.

✔ Find out in detail about the requirements of the individual fish species (see pages 10 to 21).

✔ Do not put in all the fish at once, but a few at a time.

Black Molly male (above) courts his female (below).

Three Suggestions for Stocking a 24 × 12 × 12 inch (60 × 30 × 30 cm) Aquarium

3 to 10 Days After Setting Up the Tank	10 Days After That	After Another 4 Weeks
3 Flying Foxes 1 Bristle-nosed Catfish	7 Neon Tetras, 5 Black Phantom Tetras (2 males, 3 females), 5 Harlequin Rasboras, 2 Dwarf Gourami (1 pair), 3 Armored Catfish	4 Guppies or 4 Platy (2 pairs)
3 Flying Foxes 1 Bristle-nosed Catfish	7 Zebra Danios, 5 Tiger Barbs, 3 Half-striped Barbs, 3 Armored Catfish	4 Platy or 4 Black Mollies (2 pairs)
3 Flying Foxes 1 Bristle-nosed Catfish	2 Kribensis (1 pair), 7 Black Neon Tetras, 5 Rosy Tetras or 5 Red Phantom Tetras, 3 Armored Catfish	3 Siamese Fighting Fish (1 male, 2 females) or 2 Rams (1 pair)

Two Suggestions for Stocking a 40 × 15 × 20 inch (100 × 40 × 50 cm) Aquarium

3 to 10 Days After Setting Up the Tank	10 Days After That	After Another 4 Weeks
4 to 6 Flying Foxes 1 Bristle-nosed Catfish	25 Neon Tetras or Cardinal Tetras, 7 Bleeding Heart Tetras, 5 Congo Tetras, 1 Red-tailed Black Shark, 12 Harlequin Rasboras, 10 Armored Catfish	6 Rams (3 pairs) or 2 Kribensis (1 pair), after an additional 2 weeks: 3 Angelfish
4 to 6 Flying Foxes 1 Bristle-nosed Catfish	25 Harlequin Rasboras, 10 Emperor Tetras, 10 Penguin Fish, 3 Clown Loaches, 4 Blue Gourami (2 pairs), 10 Armored Catfish	6 Rams (3 pairs), after an additional 2 weeks: 3 Angelfish

A New Idea: The Cube Aquarium

A square table is the ideal site for a cube aquarium measuring 24 × 24 × 20 inches (60 × 60 × 50 cm). Green aquatic plants are a pretty addition. Lighting is provided by a hanging lamp with 125-watt HPMV (high-pressure mercury vapor) bulb. At a distance of 20 inches (50 cm) above the water surface (table height approximatey 24 inches [60 cm] + aquarium depth 20 inches [50 cm] + distance from the water surface 20 inches [50 cm]), it illuminates a surface area of about 11 square feet (1 square meter).

Fish stocking suggestion: One Bristle-nosed Catfish, five to seven Flying Foxes, one Clown Loach (as a snail eater), up to ten Armored Catfish, three Upsidedown Catfish, ten Red Phantom Tetras, ten Black Phantom Tetras or ten Emperor Tetras, five to seven Bleeding Heart Tetras, up to three pairs of Rams, and three Angelfish (introduced after three weeks).

In an open cube aquarium, the plants can grow out of the water.

BUYING AND SETTING UP AN AQUARIUM

Anyone who buys an aquarium would like to have many years of pleasure from this new acquisition. Therefore, you should plan your purchase carefully. The right equipment ensures that fish and plants will thrive.

The Right Aquarium

The first step to becoming an aquarist is buying an aquarium. Even if aquariums seem to vary only in size, differences occur in quality. Do not be penny-wise and pound-foolish. Good, brand-name aquariums last for a long time and save you a lot of aggravation. The most common types today are all-glass aquariums, which come with or without trim.

Since an aquarium should provide a suitable habitat for plants and fish, it must not be too small. Standard tanks with a length of 24 to 50 inches (60 to 130 cm) are recommended. Children can best handle a 24-inch (60-cm) aquarium, while a tank at least 30 inches (80 cm) long would make an ideal first aquarium for adults.

Substrate

The substrate is the medium in which plant roots take hold and that stores nutrients. It also serves as a decorative and design element.

Quartz gravel in particle sizes of 0.1 to 0.2 inches (3 to 5 mm) is an ideal substrate. Coarser

Three male Guppies (**Poecilia reticulata**) *display their beautiful caudal fins.*

gravel is less suitable since it collects too much dirt and is difficult to keep clean. Pet stores carry prewashed gravel, but this must still be washed before it goes into the aquarium. Gravel must be free of calcium so it does not adversely affect the water conditions. In addition, the quartz gravel should not be too light in color or it will reflect the light too much.

Sand has two disadvantages. For instance, it gets dirty easily. In addition, plants do not grow very well in it. However, for some fish like Armored Catfish and Barbs, which like to burrow in the bottom, you can still put in a small area of sand.

Soil supplement provides aquarium plants with important nutrients. It is added to the gravel as a slow-release fertilizer when setting up the aquarium. Alternatively, it can be pressed into the substrate later as tablets.

Decorative Materials

Rocks and roots are the most important decorative objects in the aquarium. By using them, you can design the aquarium to suit your fish and construct hiding places needed by some species (for example territorial fish like Cichlids). How you decorate depends on your taste.

Shopping List for a 24-inch (60-cm) Aquarium

You can get the following basic equipment all at once. It is better to buy food and fish 3 to 10 days later.

1 all-glass aquarium (24 × 12 × 12 inches [60 × 30 × 30 cm]), with or without trim

1 sheet of expanded polystyrene 0.4 inch (10 mm) thick (only for aquariums without plastic frames)

6 bags of gravel 5.5 pounds (2.5 kg) each (grain size 0.1 to 0.2 inch [3 to 5 mm]), not too light in color)

1 package soil supplement

3 rounded pebbles or slate stones

1 flat rock or piece of slate

1 aquarium root

water conditioner

1 liquid fertilizer for later plant care

1 internal power filter with foam insert

1 automatic aquarium water heater with calibration in degrees (35-50 watts)

1 aquarium hood with integrated fluorescent bulb (15 watt), color temperature 2,700°K

1 aquarium background

1 aquarium thermometer

1 aquarium scraper (algae magnet)

1 hose for water changes, 5 feet (1.5 m) long, 0.5 to 0.6 inch (12 to 16 mm) in diameter

1 labeled, 10-quart (10 L) bucket used only for aquarium

1 timer for light

multiple outlet power strip

do not forget the plants

Rocks: Suitable types are igneous and metamorphic rocks like quartz; granite; red, green, or black slate; and calcium-free lava (not sharp edged; if necessary, break the edges with a few hammer blows).

Roots: You can use oak roots from bogs (do not remove them from the wild) or so-called bogwood (pine).

Ceramic or plastic: If the objects made of these materials do not release any harmful substances into the water, they can be used.

Background: Sheets are attached to the outside of the glass, three-dimensional dioramas are glued to the inside with spots of silicone sealant.

Things that do not belong in the aquarium: Fish can injure themselves on sharp-edged objects. Water is adversely affected by roots that come right from the woods, calcareous rocks, seashells, and fresh coconut shells.

Buying Tips

✔ Important for all decisions concerning the aquarium: Take your time. First get the aquarium along with the accessories.

✔ Very important: First set up the aquarium, then buy the fish at the earliest three, or better yet ten days later! The water needs time to mature into a habitat suitable for fish (see page 33).

✔ When in doubt, have someone explain the function of the equipment to you.

✔ Do not buy plants for the aquarium haphazardly. A planting layout ensures that you will have variety in your aquarium. Uniform vegetation without species diversity can degrade the water quality.

Safety Around the Aquarium

Water damage and insurance: The nightmare of an aquarium bursting rarely ever becomes a reality. Nevertheless, you should be prepared. The water damage that could result from an overflowing or leaky aquarium is usually quite extensive. Therefore, before purchasing your aquarium, have it included in your homeowner's or renter's insurance and find out what expenses are covered.

Protection from electric accidents: In order to provide suitable living conditions for fish and plants in the aquarium, electric appliances likes filters, heaters, and lamps are necessary. Electricity and water is a dangerous combination. Please be sure to observe the following safety precautions:

✔ When buying electric equipment, be sure that it carries the UL (Underwriters Laboratory) listing mark.

✔ Equipment for the aquarium must be labeled as being suitable for this use.

✔ Obtain a ground-fault circuit interrupter (GFCI) in the pet store or electric supply store. When connected between the power source and the appliance, it immediately interrupts the flow of electric current in the event of defects in equipment or cables.

✔ Unplug the aquarium before you work in it, or remove electric devices from the aquarium.

✔ Have repairs done only by a trained professional.

Equipment

Lighting

Fish kept in freshwater aquariums tend to come from tropical regions where lighting conditions differ from those here in North America. The light is brighter and the light intensity remains more or less constant over a period of 12 to 14 hours. Therefore, you must provide artificial lighting.

Aquarium lighting: The simplest way to light a freshwater aquarium properly is to buy an aquarium hood with one or more brackets for fluorescent bulbs. They are available for all standard tank sizes. Fluorescent bulbs produce a good light output with low energy consumption and give off very little heat. The number of bulbs depends on the depth of the water. For a 24-inch (60-cm) tank with a water depth of about 12 inches (30 cm), one bulb is sufficient. In a 40-inch (100-cm) tank with a water depth of about 15 inches (40 cm), you need two bulbs.

Red-eye Tetras (**Moenkhausia sanctaefilomenae**) *prefer the upper level of the tank.*

Color temperature: When buying bulbs, pay attention to color temperature, which is indicated by a number.

Suitable color temperatures for the aquarium are 6,000°K, 4,000°K, and 2,700°K. The warm hue of color temperature 2,700°K shows off plants especially well.

Duration of lighting: Lighting must be continuous for 12 to 14 hours. Interruptions harm the plants, which will then become stunted. In addition, interruptions will cause problems with algae growth. Therefore, you should install a timer that turns the light on and off precisely on time.

Heating

With water temperature as with light, you must bear in mind the conditions in the fish's

Every group of Tiger Barbs—about five to seven animals—has a leader.

native tropical waters. All the fish presented in this book must be kept at temperatures of 75 to 79°F (24 to 26°C).

Automatic aquarium water heaters reliably ensure a constant temperature in the aquarium. The simplest to operate are aquarium heaters with a temperature adjustment knob calibrated in degrees Farenheit (degrees Celsius). All you have to do is preselect the desired temperature, for example 75°F (24°C). The water temperature will then level out between 75 and 77°F (24 and 25°C).

Slight temperature variations of 2 to 4°F (1 to 2°C) do not harm the fish. The aquarium heater is attached vertically in one of the rear corners of the aquarium.

Tip: An alternative to the automatic heater is the cable heater, which is laid down in loops on the bottom of the aquarium and held in place with cable anchors. Do not kink the cable. Ask for advice in the pet store.

Filters

To keep an aquarium clean and the fish healthy, a filter is absolutely necessary to rid the water of waste products like fish feces, uneaten food, or decaying plant matter and then to purify it again. Different types of filters are available. Internal or external filters driven by a centrifugal pump are recommended.

Internal filters: When securely mounted, these perform just as well as external filters. Smaller models, usually placed into one of the rear corners, have a limited effect (only recommended for small tanks). In large tanks, they are useful as supplemental equipment, for example, to produce stronger currents.

External filter: It is best housed in the aquarium cabinet and is suitable for any size tank. For instructions about filter installation, see page 31.

Thermofilter: With this practical and space-saving filter, the aquarium water is first cleaned and then brought to the correct temperature.

Filter media: For the internal filter, porous foam is used (filter cartridges). The external filter uses a coarse filter substrate. Activated filter carbon is ideal for follow-up treatment when giving medications (see page 52). A wide variety of other filter media are used for different purposes or in large filters (for example, small ceramic tubes). Do not use filter floss because it compacts too quickly (except in combination with activated carbon filtration).

Checklist
Location

1 You should be able to observe your aquarium comfortably—perhaps from your favorite chair.

2 There must be enough room, if possible on the side as well, so that you can comfortably perform all maintenance tasks.

3 At least one grounded electric outlet must be near the aquarium.

4 For a 24-inch (60-cm) tank, a sturdy table will do as a base. To test if it is strong enough, try sitting on it.

5 Larger aquariums are best placed onto a special aquarium stand.

6 Windowsill locations are unsuitable; they are too bright and too hot in the summer.

7 The aquarium must have a secure place where it can remain permanently.

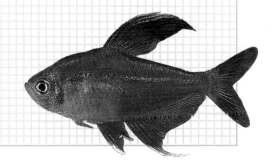

Preliminary Work

✔ Twenty-four hours before setting up, put the roots into hot water, then scrub them until all remnants of bark have been removed.

✔ To test if the tank is watertight, put it onto a level surface (balcony or basement) and fill it with water. Then rinse out the tank with lukewarm water.

✔ Wash the gravel thoroughly in a bucket—keep pouring off the dirty water and adding clean water until the water remains clear. When pouring the dirty water into a sink, hold a coarse strainer beneath it so that the drain does not get clogged.

✔ Scrub rocks with lukewarm water.

Important: Do not use any cleaning agents—the residues can poison the water.

Carefully lower the motor head straight down into position.

Put in the Substrate

Place the aquarium (a 24-inch [60-cm] tank) into its permanent location. Place tanks without trim onto a sheet of expanded polystyrene; always set aquariums with trim directly onto the base. Spread two bags of gravel evenly over the bottom of the tank, scatter substrate fertilizer over that, and add another four bags of gravel.

Rocks and roots provide wonderful hiding places.

Decorate and Partially Fill with Water

Build a cave with the rocks (pebbles, slate) in the middle part of the tank: arrange three rocks in a semicircle, lay them lightly on the gravel, and cover with a flat rock to make a cave roof. Then arrange the roots to the left or right in the gravel. They can sit at an angle on top of the cave.

Tap water containing a water conditioner can be used to fill the aquarium for the first time. Only very hard tap water should be conditioned further. Fill the tank about one-third full with water: lay a piece of polystyrene (8 × 12 inches [20 × 30 cm]) into one corner of the tank. Pour in the water with a watering can reserved for this purpose. Let the water flow over the poly-

styrene so that the substrate is not stirred. When about one-third of the water has been added, put in the plants (see page 34).

Install the Equipment

Before you attach the filter and aquarium heater, slowly fill the tank about two-thirds full with water, adding the water conditioner bit by bit. Be careful! Do not wash out any of the plants. Replant any that are accidentally dislodged. Install the filter in the left rear corner and the heater in the right rear corner with their suction cups. Position the suction cups of the heater as indicated by the markings in the upper third of the device. Attach the thermometer to the left front aquarium glass.

Now carefully pour in the remaining one-third of the water containing conditioner. Fasten the background to the outside of the aquarium with adhesive tape. Carefully place the hood with the fluorescent bulb onto the aquarium. Plug in the equipment, turn on the light and timer.

Tip: Wait until the cloudiness of the water has completely disappeared before adding the fish (see "During the Waiting Period," page 33).

Install the External Filter

The installation of an external filter looks rather complicated at first. However, if you carry out the steps in the order described here and pay attention to a few points, the filter will function right away. Proceed as follows:

✔ Attach the filter hoses to the filter canister.

✔ Open the filter canister, and add the filter media between the filter strainers or chambers. Do not put the substrate into bags, do not use filter floss.

✔ Moisten the O-ring, set the motor head with gasket onto the filter, and clamp shut (see illustration, page 30 top).

✔ Connect the filter with the intake tube (if possible using couplings).

✔ Apply suction briefly to the return line using your mouth or a mechanical siphon starter in order to get the water into the filter canister (the canister will slowly fill with water).

✔ Connect the return line with the spray bar. The spray bar should be mounted below the water level with the nozzles oriented in such a way that the stream of water flows horizontally from the back to the front of the tank.

✔ Wait until the rising water has forced the air out of the filter into the return line. When it no longer gurgles, the air is out.

✔ Now plug it in. The filter will start up immediately. Should you hear hissing noises, that is the air escaping from the new filter material. If the motor makes rattling noises, unplug it and plug it in again.

Tip: Except during aquarium maintenance, never turn off the filter.

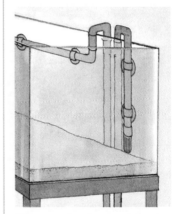

The spray bar is mounted onto the rear wall.

Diamond Tetras (**Moenkhausia pittieri**) *are placid animals whose brilliance does credit to their name.*

Other Accessories

A thermometer is absolutely necessary in order to monitor the water temperature regularly. All you need is a simple aquarium thermometer fastened with suction cups to the inside of the glass opposite the heater.

Timers are highly recommended to maintain a constant day length (12 to 14 hours a day). Then you do not run the risk of someday forgetting to turn the light on or off.

Carbon dioxide (CO$_2$) fertilization equipment encourages plant growth. A diffusion bell or a CO$_2$ diffuser are recommended. These devices, which are simple to operate and moderately priced, keep CO$_2$ on hand. Beginners should not use continuous injection devices, since overdosing can easily occur with improper use.

Aquarium vacuums are practical for cleaning the substrate.

Algae magnets or aquarium scrapers make the job of cleaning much easier.

An Oxydator is a special device that can be used to add oxygen to the water. It requires no electric supply. It is very helpful when more oxygen is needed quickly in the event of an aquarium breakdown or illness among the fish.

An aquarium stand is definitely recommended as a base for larger, heavier aquariums. Because of its design, such a stand is able to support heavy loads. Furthermore, you can easily house the external filter and accessories inside it.

During the Waiting Period

Once the tank is completely set up, it must, as mentioned, be broken in for a little while. Let the filter and heater run, set the timer for the aquarium lighting to a 12- to 14-hour cycle (from 8 A.M. to 10 P.M., for example), and do not add any fish as long as the water is still cloudy. For the sake of the fish, be patient.

However, even without containing fish, you can marvel at much in the aquarium over the next few days. The water seems cloudy, often even brownish, it is full of air bubbles, and a whitish slime may cover the glass. These signs are completely normal. Further development will show you how the water becomes a suitable habitat for fish.

Cloudiness of the water is caused by the slow-release fertilizer as it dissolves. Later, it will be removed by the plants and in part by the filter. Add the fish only after the water has cleared.

Brownish water frequently results from roots used as decorations. Roots release tannic or humic acid, which gives the water a brownish color. However, the acid does no further harm, and the color almost completely disappears later during regular water changes.

White slime on the glass is due to colonization by bacteria that feed on free protein in the water. This slime is later eaten by snails or removed when the glass is cleaned. Cleaning the glass as a precaution is unnecessary.

TIP

Help for Fish Put in Too Soon

You have put your fish in too soon if you happen to notice the following:

✔ The fish stay below the water surface and do not go into the cover provided by the plants.

✔ The fish hang vertically and gasp for air.

✔ The fish wobble and spin around the long axis.

✔ The fish swim erratically.

If these signs occur, you should take the following steps:

1. Every three days, change one-third of the water and add water conditioner.

2. Check to see if the filter is letting enough water through. If there is only a trickle, you must clean it (see "Filter Maintenance," page 43).

3. Feed only a little and then only flake food; under no circumstances offer frozen food or add vitamins to the aquarium water.

4. Do not fertilize the aquarium plants until the tank is broken in again.

5. After about two weeks, the aquarium has, so to speak, settled down. Now you can resume the normal maintenance cycle! (see "Maintenance Schedule for Routine Tasks," page 45).

6. Add new fish only after another two weeks have passed.

Decorating with Plants

✔ The requirements of the plants should more or less correspond with the requirements of your fish.

✔ Find out how large the plants grow. Otherwise, in small tanks, you must constantly be cutting back overgrown plants, which will eventually harm the plants.

✔ Carpet-forming plants belong in the foreground and taller ones on the sides or in the background. A very decorative specimen plant can also brighten up the middle ground. When placing the plants, make sure that you leave enough room for the fish to swim.

Putting in the Plants

Bunch plants: To plant, lay the stem onto the gravel, and weigh it down with a large pebble. Thus anchored, the plant will simultaneously send out roots from several leaf nodes and take hold very quickly.

Rooted plants:
These are often sold in miniature pots with rock wool. To take out, turn the pot over, tap it gently against the edge of a table, and remove the plant. Shorten the roots with scissors to a maximum of 1 inch (3 cm) long (never pinch them

To root, weigh down the plant with a rock.

off with your fingers!). Then poke a hole into the gravel with your finger, put the plant in so that the crown is not buried, and fill in the planting hole again (never press down hard).

Plant Care

In order for the plants in the aquarium to remain biologically active, produce oxygen, remove waste products, and develop their other

1 *Giant Eel Grass*
  (Vallisneria gigantea
2 *Red Amazon Swordp*
  (Echinodorus osiris
3 *Java Fern*
  (Microsorium ptero
4 *Giant Indian Water*
  (Nomaphila stricta)
5 *New Zealand Grass*
  (Lilaeopsis novae ze

Putting in rooted plants: 1. Poke a hole into the substrate with your finger. 2. Set the plant into this hole.

water-purifying characteristics, they must receive optimal care.

Fertilization: For healthy growth, plants need additional nutrients. For this purpose, aquarium plant fertilizers, iron fertilizers, and the CO_2 equipment mentioned on page 32 are available. When fertilizing, you should pay attention to the following:

✔ Carefully follow the dosage instructions given in the directions.

✔ Fertilize for the first time during setup then after every water change.

✔ Liquid fertilizers can also be used alone in aquariums without slow-release fertilizer in the substrate.

✔ Use a CO_2-supplying system, see page 32.

Pruning and thinning: If plants grow too rampantly, they must be supported or thinned. Fish out floating plants occasionally; any dead plant matter not siphoned up during water changes can be removed by hand.

Pruning Bunch Plants

When you notice that a plant has stretched out along the water surface, you should shorten it.

Cut off two-thirds with a sharp knife.

To do so, cut off two-thirds of the plant with scissors or a sharp knife. After just 14 days, you will discover new shoots.

If you cut off too little, the plant will send out runners directly under the water surface. These give a lot of shade and prevent the lower leaves from receiving light. The plant loses its lower leaves and becomes bare. Even improperly pruned plants can be brought back into shape again. Simply bend down the stem to the bottom, and weigh it down with a stone. As soon as the stem has taken root, separate it from the parent plant. Now the plant can grow bushy. If you put the cut end of the stem under a stone, it will soon take root.

The plant will then grow more luxuriantly.

ROUTINE AQUARIUM MAINTENANCE

After your aquarium has been set up and the fish have begun to feel at home, the aquarium requires only a little care. If you know about some of the processes in the aquarium, you can carry out the regular tasks more easily.

The Water Habitat

Water is for fish what air is for people. Just as we feel best in good clean air, our fish need good, clean water. This is achieved through regular maintenance. In order to understand this, you must know what actually constitutes good water for fish. The following checklist names the critical parameters involved in creating and maintaining a good water environment in an aquarium:

✔ acidity of the water (pH value),
✔ water hardness,
✔ nitrite-nitrate levels, and
✔ atmospheric gases dissolved in the water—oxygen (O_2) and carbon dioxide (CO_2).

Acidity of the Water

The acidity of the water is expressed by the pH value. The pH scale ranges from 0 to 14. Neutrality is assigned a value of 7. Values from 0 to 6.9 mean that the water is acidic, values from 7.1 to 14 indicate that the water is alkaline. Most tropical ornamental fish prefer a range between 6.5 and 7.5. Naturally, some fish are exceptions (see "Species of Aquarium Fish,"

Splendid male Cockatoo Dwarf Cichlid in a display posture.

pages 10 to 21), but the majority of fish mentioned in this book are happy in this range.

Measuring the pH: The pet store sells various reagents with which the pH can be easily determined.

Changing the pH: In most cases, water comes out of the tap with a pH value slightly above 7. Thus, as a rule, you can use tap water in setting up your aquarium. Measure the pH after a few days, though. If it lies in the specified range, the fish can be added.

If necessary, the pH can also be lowered artificially. The simplest way is by adding pH-lowering agents like pH Minus or pHkH Minus (pH Down) and the somewhat more difficult to use peat extracts. Be careful. The brown coloration absorbs light that bottom-dwelling plants require. Checking the pH during and also one to two days after adjusting it is important.

Tip: Monitoring the pH is part of routine maintenance.

Water Hardness

Total or general hardness of water is measured in parts per million of calcium carbonate (ppm). The levels of hardness are differentiated as follows:

very soft = less than 75 ppm
soft = between 75 and 150 ppm
medium = between 150 and 220 ppm
hard = between 220 and 360 ppm
very hard = more than 360 ppm.

You can find out the hardness of your tap water at your local water authority. If the hardness is in the soft to medium hard range, most fish are happy in it. If the water is harder, you must soften it.

Reducing water hardness: For the beginner, the simplest method to reduce water hardness is to dilute the hard aquarium water with distilled water, monitoring it constantly, until the desired value is attained. Plants and fish cannot tolerate having the hardness reduced too quickly.

With his brilliant colors, the Cockatoo Dwarf Cichlid is a beautiful addition to the aquarium.

Tip: For beginners, do not use the peat filtration technique used by experienced aquarists (it darkens the water too much, and plant growth suffers as a consequence) or the water-softening devices available in pet stores.

Water conditions can be slowly regulated and stabilized by the addition of CO_2 (see page 32) and iron fertilizer for fast-growing plants.

Waste Products in the Aquarium

Even in well-maintained aquariums, waste materials constantly accumulate, namely organic waste products coming from fish excrement, excess food, as well as decaying plant and animal matter. In the aquarium, these waste products are continually being transformed by bacteria present in the substrate, the filter, and the water. The process generates nitrite, which is toxic for fish. Nitrite is then transformed into the less harmful nitrate. In this aerobic process carried out by the bacteria, the most important helpers are the plants. This means that as long as enough oxygen is available, your tank is well stocked with a variety of plants, and the filter is functioning properly, you will usually not encounter any problems with the nitrite-nitrate levels.

Dangerous conditions for the fish arise only if the fish live in a tank where the plants grow poorly or that has too little plant diversity or is very dirty. In such tanks, the nitrite-nitrate levels get out of whack. At first, it does not necessarily have any effect on the well-being of the fish. However, the moment enough oxygen is no longer available or maintenance tasks are undertaken, such as changing the water or cleaning the filter, signs of poisoning appear in the fish. These signs include the fish gasping for air at the water surface and refusing their food. If you have allowed things to get this far in the tank, you must now take action very quickly. In small tanks, cleaning the entire tank and setting it up again is best for the fish.

Emergency Program for Neglected Aquariums

The following measures must be carried out for two to three weeks:

✔ Supply oxygen constantly.

✔ Carefully loosen the gravel with your fingers so that any trapped fermentation gas escapes. Do not stir up the bottom in the process.

✔ Change one-third of the water immediately and then every week.

✔ Clean the filter immediately and then again after 14 days.

✔ Do not feed the fish for the first three days.

✔ Add Biocoryn H3 (a biological water conditioner) to the water, following the manufacturer's directions.

✔ After three weeks, switch to normal aquarium maintenance.

✔ As a rule, this emergency program helps. However, some fish and plants may not survive the procedure.

Tip: All problems caused by organic waste products can be prevented by properly caring for water, filter, and plants.

The barbels allow the Corydoras to explore its surroundings by touch.

Oxygen and Carbon Dioxide

The gases oxygen and carbon dioxide play a major role in the life of the aquarium inhabitants.

Oxygen (O_2): This gas is required by animals and plants for respiration. Respiration is the process where an organism, like fish, extracts energy from food. Good plant growth and agitation of the water surface by the filter provide the most natural oxygen supply.

If supplying additional oxygen (in other words, good aeration) becomes necessary, you can do this using airstones and diffusers. The best option, because it works the fastest, is the Oxydator. When using it, follow the manufacturer's instructions precisely.

When there is a lack of oxygen in the aquarium, the fish breath heavily and swim just beneath the water surface. If this occurs, you must supply oxygen immediately. If the behavior of the fish does not change after that, you

Half-striped Barbs (**Puntius semifasciolatus**) *are lively schooling fish.*

should check to see if they might be suffering from poisoning due to poor water conditions and then take the appropriate measures.

Carbon dioxide (CO_2): This gas is a by-product of fish respiration. In addition, it is also produced by the bacteria present in the aquarium filter and substrate. CO_2 is an important plant nutrient. Since the plants in the aquarium consume large quantities of CO_2, it must be kept in reserve as well. This is done with the simple CO_2 devices recommended on page 32 for beginners (diffusion bell or CO_2 diffuser).

Naturally, even better plant growth can be achieved using mechanical injection during the day. However, the unused CO_2 must then be driven out again at night by means of artificial aeration.

Cleaning the Aquarium

Before you begin cleaning, please be sure to pull out all the electric plugs (see "Protection from Electric Accidents," page 27).

Changing the water: You should change one-third of the water once a week. (Do not change more of the water each week. If you do, the water quality will change too much). Theoretically, you could simply bail out the water. However, the task is faster if you use a siphon hose and a bucket.

To change the water, follow these directions. First, take a hose 5 feet (1.5 m) long with a diameter of 0.5 to 0.6 inches (12 to 16 mm), and fill it with water at the tap or from a filled washbasin. Then close the ends of the hose with your thumbs, hold one end up above in the aquarium and the other in the bucket down below. This difference in height is important, otherwise the siphon will not work. First open the end in the aquarium, then the one in the bucket, and the water will begin to flow immediately. The suction is strong enough to vacuum up leftover food, mulm, and algae along with the water. While you guide the hose through the aquarium with one hand, the other hand should continue to hold the end of the hose in the bucket. There you can stop the flow of water quickly in case a fish threatens to get near the end of the hose or is even sucked up into the hose.

Should that happen anyway, then pour the water in the bucket through a net and put the fish back into the aquarium.

Siphoning up mulm: You will notice that over time, a brown layer of mulm settles on the bottom of the aquarium, especially in the corners. Mulm is a mixture of dead plant matter and fish wastes. It should be removed from time to time because too much oxygen is consumed during bacterial decomposition of the mulm.

Bleeding Heart Tetras are easily recognized by their brilliant red spot.

You can siphon up mulm during water changes or use a so-called aquarium vacuum. Move the vacuum carefully back and forth over the gravel. Mulm and water go into the bucket, the heavier gravel falls back to the bottom. Never go too deeply into the substrate, or you will destroy the fine roots of the plants, which are essential for their survival.

Cleaning the glass: Get into the habit of cleaning the aquarium glass inside and out once a week.

To clean the outside, you can simply wipe off the glass of the aquarium with a damp cloth.

A practical solution for cleaning the inside of the glass is the so-called algae magnet. If you use an aquarium scraper with a razor blade, be careful not to cut into the silicone sealant that holds the aquarium glass together.

Tip: Do not use chemicals to clean the glass.

Algae Control

Algal Species	Appearance	Countermeasures
Beard algae	Dark brown, very tenacious, frequently on Java Fern	Cut off heavily infested leaves, introduce algae eaters like Half-striped, Ruby, or Tiger Barbs.
Brush algae	Dark brown, partly free swimming, partly on rocks or plants	Siphon up gravel and free-floating algae, discard gravel. Introduce algae eaters like Flying Foxes, Half-striped, or Ruby Barbs; Black Molly; Guppy; or Platy.
Diatoms	Dark green spots on the upper surfaces of leaves, often on Anubias and Echinodorus species, mostly on old leaves	Do not remove infested leaves. Introduce algae eaters like Bushy-mouthed Catfish or Whiptail Catfish.
Blue-green algae	Bluish black to dark green, can easily be wiped off, algae smell like ammonium chloride	Add iron fertilizer. (Introduce algae eaters like Japanese Bitterling.) Do not let temperature rise above 75°F (24°C).
Brown algae	Light brownish coating on leaves, rocks, glass	Introduce algae eaters like Suckermouths and Bushy-mouthed Catfish.
Filamentous algae	Ensnare leaf stalks and then everything else with a cottony web	Add iron fertilizer. Introduce algae eaters like Flying Foxes, Black Molly, and Sailfin Molly. Put in fast-growing plants like Waterweed.
Volvox algae	Water colored pea green	Do not change the water. Use a diatom filter or UV light (ask the pet dealer for advice). As a supporting measure, use an Oxydator.
	Slimy, bright green coating over everything in the aquarium	Change water, put in fast-growing plants like Waterweed and Water Wisteria.
	Fuzzy dark brown coating on upper surfaces of leaves that cannot be wiped off	Introduce algae eaters like Flying Foxes, Bushy-mouthed Catfish, Whiptail Catfish, Guppy, or Black Molly.

Tip: When you introduce algae eaters, do not feed them for 8 days.

Filter Maintenance

Filter materials with a rather coarse structure like foam and porous biosubstrate are primarily simple mechanical filter media. These are colonized over time by bacteria. The bacteria within these filters break down the trapped dirt. In the process, plant nutrients and carbon dioxide (CO_2), among other things, are released. This process turns the filter medium into a biological filter. *Bio* means involving living organisms. In the case of aquarium filters, microorganisms (bacteria) are involved. Therefore, in biological filters, microorganisms take over the job of cleaning. However, this functions in the aquarium only if the filter is properly maintained.

Maintenance of the internal filter: Every two to four weeks (depending on fish stock), wash out the filter foam with lukewarm water (without the addition of cleaners), squeeze it out, and reuse it. Replace the foam when it loses its shape.

Maintenance of the external filter: Every three to four months, wash out the substrate with lukewarm water until the water remains clear. Follow the manufacturer's instructions. When changing the filter medium, reuse some of the old substrat, which contains bacteria. Doing so will allow the bacterial population to colonize the filter material right away.

TIP

Snails as Scavengers

They get rid of leftover food, dying plant matter, algae, and dead animals. You would probably be surprised to discover snails in your aquarium without having bought any, but new aquarium plants usually have some snail eggs hanging on them.

If snails get out of hand, it is generally because of overfeeding. The more food available, the more they reproduce. If that is the case, you can easily set up a kind of snail trap. First feed the fish, then put one to two food tablets onto a flat rock. After a while, more and more snails will show up there. All you have to do is collect them and preferably add them to the compost pile.

Tip: In order to preserve the filter bacteria, never rinse out the filter material with water hotter than lukewarm (about 86°F [30°C]). Never boil or disinfect the filter

Algae in the Aquarium

Aquariums without algae do not exist. Algae are as much a part of an aquarium as the plants, fish, and bacteria. In a well-maintained

Agassiz's Dwarf Cichlid (**Apistogramma agassizi**) *loves roots and caves where it can hide.*

CARE DURING VACATION

If you cannot rely on anyone to take care of your aquarium during your absence, you should make a few preparations:

✔ *For a few weeks before the start of your vacation, do not add any new fish. Otherwise, you have no control over problems that may arise.*

✔ *Fourteen days before the beginning of your vacation, install an automatic feeder. Feed using only this so that the fish get used to it and you can gauge the correct portion size and frequency. If necessary, prolong the intervals between feedings so that the food is really eaten.*

✔ *About five days before departing, change one-third of the water. This can conveniently siphon up troublesome mulm.*

✔ *Three days before departing, clean the internal filter. External filters can take care of the water for up to four months with no problems.*

✔ *One day before departing, turn on the timer and check all equipment.*

✔ *If anyone will be checking on your aquarium, leave behind the telephone number of the pet store for emergencies.*

aquarium, algae are kept in check by algae eaters. Algae become a problem when they suddenly get out of hand and become clearly visible. Increased algal growth is a warning sign that means something could be wrong in the aquarium. You should then take the appropriate measures to control the algae. Algal control does not mean, however, that you reach for the appropriate chemicals. Instead, you must first find out what is causing the excessive algal growth and do something about it. If too many things are not wrong at once, the algal problem usually clears up by itself as soon as you have eliminated the causes. Otherwise, you must institute specific algal control measures (see table, page 42).

You need to find the causes for the increased algal growth. In order to track them down, you must check over the aquarium.

✔ Is the filter clean?

✔ Is the duration of lighting correct? Could any of the fluorescent bulbs need to be replaced?

✔ Have you changed the water regularly?

✔ Is the temperature correct?

✔ Are the carbon dioxide (CO_2) and oxygen (O_2) levels OK?

✔ Are the nitrite-nitrate levels OK?

✔ Is the pH correct?

✔ Is the water hardness OK?

✔ Are there enough algae eaters in the aquarium?

For all the questions that you have answered with *no*, you must remedy the problem and wait.

Maintenance Schedule for Routine Tasks

Tip: In order not to disturb the fish too much, perform no more than one maintenance task per day.

Daily	Inspect electric equipment, check temperature, check health of fish (see page 51), replenish CO_2, and feed (see page 48).
Weekly	Clean glass (see page 41), change one-third of water, siphon up mulm in the process (see page 41), remove loose leaves, test and adjust water conditions, add water conditioner, and fertilize plants (1 tablet per 50 quarts [50 L] aquarium water).
Monthly	Prune plants (see page 35) and clean internal filter (see page 43).
Every 3 months	Clean external filter (see page 43).
Every 6 months	Replace hoses (they become hard and are then no longer reliable) and replace fluorescent bulbs. For double-bulb hoods it is easier on the plants if you change only one at a time (first one and then the other 3 months later).
As required	Siphon up leftover food, remove dead plant matter, and gather snails and remove dead fish.

The Right Food

In earlier times, feeding fish with food caught in the wild with his or her own hands was a point of honor for the aquarist. The aquarist always took a net along on walks in order to fish for water fleas, mosquito larvae, or fresh-water shrimp in the nearest pond or stream. Fishing for food in the wild is nearly impossible today. Fewer and fewer suitable bodies of water are available. For the most part, they are polluted, or fishing from them is generally prohibited. Conservation laws forbid the removal of small creatures, including tadpoles and all other larvae of newts and salamanders. Furthermore, the danger of introducing pathogens into the aquarium is enormous. You can easily give your fish a varied diet using the food sold in pet stores instead of catching their food yourself.

Dried food is available as flakes, tablets, and granules. It contains sufficient amounts of all the important nutrients for your fish as well as adequate fiber (for stimulating bowel function). Dried food constitutes the staple in your fish's diet.

✔ Flake food comes in various sizes. Fry and small fish species get small flakes, large fish receive large flakes, the medium-sized flakes are accepted by all. When choosing which type of flake food to purchase, pay attention to the special nutritional requirements of your fish. Species that prefer vegetarian fare need flake food that contains a lot of vegetable matter.

✔ Tablets for bottom-feeding fish can simply be allowed to sink to the bottom of the tank. Tablets are also available that can be stuck to the aquarium glass, where they are available for all fish.

✔ Granules, so-called crumb foods (a highly nutritious food), are not accepted by most fish right away. However, after a while, fish become accustomed to it. Feeding this alternatively with flake food is best.

Frozen food is a good substitute for live food because it consists of frozen invertebrates like mosquito larvae, water fleas, and others. Through the freezing process, any germs present are killed. This is a nutritious supplement to dried food. Frozen food must be kept in the freezer, and you should take out only as much as you will be feeding right away.

Freeze-dried food consists of invertebrates that have been frozen and then dried in a special process. It is suitable as a supplemental food.

Vitamin concentrates are a very important addition. Adding a few drops regularly (dripped onto the frozen food) meets the requirements of the fish.

Unsuitable Foods

Some foods appear to be suitable for fish at first glance, but can do the fish more harm than good.

✔ Tubifex (sludgeworms) live in the mud of heavily polluted waters and can cause disease.

✔ Kitchen scraps, such as white bread or rolled oats, do not belong in the aquarium since they can rapidly degrade the water quality.

✔ Feeding lettuce and spinach leaves is not for beginners. Giving plant eaters vegetarian food from the pet store is better.

✔ Live food is sold in many pet stores or through specialized aquarium magazines. In most cases, these are cultures of enchytraeids, small white worms. They are found underneath flagstones in the yard. They can be cultured using cooked cereal. However, the beginner can easily makes mistakes when processing and create a danger for the fish—allowing pathogens into the aquarium. Therefore, to avoid this very great danger, postpone culturing until you have acquired more experience.

Male Swordtails are especially spirited and lively.

First Aid for Breakdowns in the Aquarium

Sign	Cause	Remedy
Filter noise noticeable from 1 yard (1 m) away, drop in performance.	1. Filter dirty 2. Impeller shaft worn out or fermentation gas escaping. 3. Sand dust or unwashed filter material.	1. Change cartridge, replace hoses. 2. Replace magnet, impeller shaft, and bearings. 3. Wash out or change filter material.
Brownish green water, fish swimming at the water surface.		Change one-third of the water, increase oxygen level. Wash out filter material, connect filter, and do not feed for 3 days.
Water cloudy white, clear in the mornings, white clouds in the evenings under the fluorescent light, fish at the water surface.	Bacterial turbidity, bacteria sink to the bottom at night.	Siphon up mulm and leftover food, increase oxygen level with Oxydator. Kill bacteria with molluscicide. Follow instructions very carefully! Do not feed for 3 days until breathing is normal. Clean filter 10 days later.
Water clear but all fish at the water surface.	Temperature too high, usually in summer.	Do not change the water (shock), check the heater! Immediately increase oxygen with Oxydator. Do not feed for 3 days.
Damp around the aquarium. Glass and silicone sealant undamaged.	1. Water level too low, filter spray escaping. 2. Filter hose leaky. 3. Diffuser connected incorrectly. 4. Defective gasket.	1. Refill evaporated water. 2. Replace hoses. 3. Check direction of nozzle discharge. 4. Replace gasket.
Drop in temperature.	Heater defective or room temperature too low.	Not dangerous! Replace heater. Room temperature should not be below 64°F (18°C).
Water cloudy.	Feeding too much.	Clean filter, vacuum substrate, change 90 percent of the water, clean the filter.
Water clear, air bubbles rising from the bottom.	Fermentation gas in the substrate due to uneaten food.	Loosen the substrate so that the gas can escape.
1. Foam on the water surface. 2. Fluff in the water.	1. Bubble nest? 2. Protein foam caused by food.	1. Do not disturb the bubble nest. 2. Clean the filter, otherwise this is not harmful.

Tip: When doing any work in the aquarium, please be sure to pull the plug.

Important Rules for Feeding

1. Feed only when you have the time to observe whether all the fish are eating. Refusal of food is a sure sign of illness.

2. Feed only as much as will be eaten right away. The food should not sink to the bottom. Exception: specific feeding of bottom-dwelling fish with food tablets that must sink to the bottom.

3. Provide a variety of foods.

4. First feed flakes as the staple diet and then frozen or freeze-dried food as treats.

5. Never feed right after you have turned on the light in the aquarium. Thirty minutes later, your fish will be fully awake.

6. Never feed right after you have been working in the aquarium (changing the water, cleaning the glass, or the like).

7. Do not crumble up the flake food; the fish should work for their food.

8. The same person should always take care of the feeding.

9. Never switch off the filter when feeding. If flakes get into the filter, the portion was too large. Food drawn into the filter has an adverse effect on it. (In this case, clean the filter.)

10. For an extended absence, it is advisable to install an automatic feeder as described on page 44. Never use time-

An automatic feeder can provide food for about 14 days.

release food. It pollutes the water.

Mouth positions

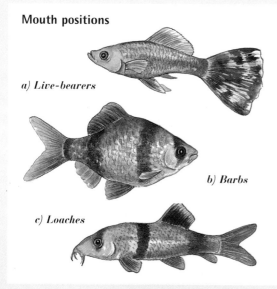

a) Live-bearers

b) Barbs

c) Loaches

In the course of evolution, the various mouth positions have adapted to different eating habits and indicate the food requirements of particular fish species.

✔ Live-bearers (see Figure a) have a superior mouth and eat mosquito larvae from the surface in the wild.

✔ Barbs (see Figure b) feel around with their barbels in the loose substrate for things to eat.

✔ Loaches (see Figure c) eat snails out of the shells by using their inferior or downward-turned mouth.

How to Feed

Scatter flakes, granules, and freeze-dried food onto the water by dispensing the food through the feeding hole in the cover of the aquarium. Stick food tablets to the glass or drop them into the water.

Frozen food is sold in tablet form, divided into 0.6 cubic inch (1 cm³) cubes. For smaller fish, which are in no danger of swallowing an entire cube, drop the frozen cube into the water. The cube will float on the surface, thaw slowly, and seem to move in the process. For this reason, frozen food is eaten even by fish who otherwise react only to the movement of their prey. For large fish, thaw the food in a dish before feeding. Otherwise, the fish would swallow the frozen cube, and that could lead to gastrointestinal problems. With open cubes, you can feed in two corners so that one fish cannot eat everything.

The Right Amount of Food

Feeding too little rather than too much is better. Constantly overfed animals are very susceptible to disease. Follow these basic rules to determine the right amount:

✔ Offer only as much food as your fish will eat in a very short time. Flakes should sink no deeper than one-third of the depth of the tank (provide bottom-dwelling fish with tablet foods). Then no leftover food will be present that would otherwise degrade the water quality.

✔ Feed several small portions in succession.

✔ If you are at home during the day, you can spread out the portions over the day. In case you can feed only in the mornings and evenings, you should be sure to take your time and feed slowly and in small helpings.

Tip: If your hand ever slips while feeding and you put too much food into the aquarium, siphon up the food just as you do mulm during water changes (see page 41). Over the next few days, wash out the filter, otherwise it could be adversely affected by leftover food.

Fish surround tablet food stuck to the aquarium glass.

*Luxuriant plant growth: Dwarf Anubias and
Cryptocorynes among pieces of Bogwood.*

Prevention Is the Best Cure

Disease-causing organisms—parasites,
bacteria, and viruses—are found in every
aquarium, brought in by new fish and plants.
Whether or not disease breaks out depends
on the resistance of your fish. Poor living
conditions weaken the resistance of the
animals. Therefore, maintaining the health
of the fish and the aquarium as a whole is
important. Use the time spent feeding to
observe the fish. Now and then, take a good
hard look at the aquarium. The earlier you
notice changes, the more effectively you can
take action.

What to Do in Case of Disease

Diseases can spread quickly, therefore you
must take remedial measures at once. The following tips should help you in this regard:
✔ In many cases, the pet dealer can give you
further assistance quickly and competently.
✔ Note changes in behavior and signs of
disease so that you can provide the most
accurate possible description of the disease.
✔ Do not resort to medications
indiscriminately. A so-called broad-spectrum
treatment with a medication that is supposed
to be good for everything is of little use. For
successful treatment, you need a medication
specifically intended for the disease. The pet
dealer will help you choose it.
✔ When administering medications, follow the
dosage guidelines exactly.

For the dosage, you must know how much water is in your tank. To calculate the number of gallons of water in a rectangular aquarium:

a) measure the aquarium length, width, and height in inches;

b) multiply the length × height × width;

c) divide by 231.

Tip: Never use medications and water conditioners together. Otherwise, the effect of the medication would be largely neutralized.

✔ Provide a high concentration of oxygen (see page 40).

✔ Clean the filter (do not use activated carbon filtration at the same time medications are being administered).

✔ Try to determine the causes and, if possible, correct them.

Tip: The entire aquarium must be treated. In most cases, transferring sick fish to a quarantine tank does little good since even apparently healthy fish may already be infected.

Supporting measure: A type of sauna method often works wonders. When the temperature is raised, the pathogenic organisms multiply, a full outbreak of the disease occurs and the medication can reach all pathogens before they encyst again. This is how it is done:

1. Change one-third of the water. When doing this, do not add any conditioner since the substances contained in it combine with the drugs and neutralize the effect of the drugs.

2. Raise the temperature while simultaneously increasing the oxygen level by a total of 2°F (4°C). Do not do this all at once. Raise the temperature by 1°F (2°C) on each of two consecutive days. The maximum possible temperature in the average aquarium should be 50°F (32°C).

3. Administer the medication at the indicated dosage. A dosage that is too low leads to the development of resistant pathogenic strains.

Checklist
Signs of Disease

1 Holes eaten into the head, whitish film around the mouth.

2 Eyes clouded or protruding.

3 Gills inflamed, brightly colored, worms hanging from them; gill covers flared out, white spots.

4 Fins ragged or shortened, cotton-like growths, white spots.

5 Scales sticking out from the body; blisters; ulcers; changes in color; heavy secretion of mucus; white spots; red, open sores.

6 Anal region is swollen; worms hanging out; long, stringy, or slimy feces.

7 Abnormal behavior including loss of appetite, rapid gill movement, gasping for air under the surface of the water, darting about wildly, jumping, twitching fins, scraping against objects, fins held close to the body, shimmying, twisting, swaying, wobbling.

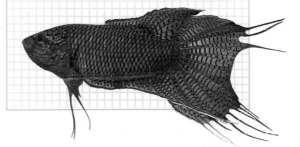

4. Do not feed for three or four days.

5. As a rule, eight days after beginning treatment, the external signs of the disease will have disappeared. Then lower the temperature again, feed normally, and give increased amounts of vitamins. Apart from that, leave the aquarium alone.

6. After another eight days, change one-third of the water and add water conditioner.

7. Check the filter to see if enough water is flowing through it.

Steps After Administering Medications

After treatment with medications, it may be necessary (for example if the water is discolored) to filter the water over activated carbon. Activated filter carbon is a chemical filter medium that changes the composition of the water.

Use: Put the dry activated carbon into a filter bag and be sure to cover with filter floss. This traps the carbon dust. The effect of the activated carbon is exhausted after about a week. Discard the carbon afterward. Do not reuse it!

Tip: Use activated carbon filtration only for the purpose mentioned since essential substances such as water conditioner and nutrients are also removed in the process.

Poisoning

Often the cause of abnormal behavior in fish is not a disease but rather poor water conditions or toxins.

1. Symptoms: Loss of color, wobbling, swimming erratically near the water surface, and twisting around the longitudinal axis.

Cause: Poisoning due to cleaning agents in the bucket, too much fertilizer, hair spray or pesticides, or water from desalinization plants.

Remedy: Change up to 80 percent of the water. Clean the filter! Add water conditioner with protective slime coating additive. Do not feed! Increase oxygen by using the Oxydator.

2. Symptoms: Loss of color, clouding of the skin covering the eyes and body, protruding eyes, rapid breathing, and fish lying quietly at an angle or on their sides.

Cause: Slow poisoning due to unfavorable water conditions such as excessively high nitrite-nitrate levels, high pH, fermentation gas in the substrate, unsuitable decorations, and moving the fish improperly.

Remedy: Change one-third of the water. Add Biocoryn H3 (a biological water conditioner). Provide oxygen. Eliminate the causes of the slow poisoning.

Plants are beautiful and useful: Water Hyssop (**Bacopa amplexicaulis**).

The Most Common Fish Diseases

Signs of Disease	Diagnosis	Treatment
Fish covered with white spots, loss of appetite, shimmying, twitching	White spot	With appropriate medications and supporting measures.
Fish swells and looks like it will burst, scales stick out	Edema caused by bacteria, improper diet	Difficult. If possible, isolate the affected fish. Stimulate metabolism using salt at 0.04 ounces per quart (1 g/L), increase oxygen level and temperature. Medicate!
Cottonlike, funguslike growths	Fungal infection following damage to the mucous coat	Appropriate medications. Increase oxygen level, change one-third of the water without conditioner, add vitamins. Clean filter after treatment.
Sudden appearance of tiny spots, easily visible from the front; spots more yellowish than white	Velvet disease	With appropriate medications and supporting measures (see page 50).
Loss of appetite, color changes, slimy whitish feces, holes in the head	Hole-in-the-head disease, almost exclusively in cichlids	Increase oxygen level. Slowly raise temperature to 50°F (33°C), as long as all fish tolerate this temperature. Medications if necessary.
Rapid breathing; scraping the head against objects; sudden protrusion of the mouth; colorless, wormlike flukes hang from the gills	Gill flukes	Increase oxygen level. Treatment with appropriate medications.
Abnormally protruding eyes	Pop eye (exophthalmus) due to poor water quality, parasites	Increase oxygen level, clean filter, change one-third of water every 3 days until water conditions are normal. Add conditioner, do not feed for 2 to 3 days.
Fins become ragged and necrotic, colors fade	Fin rot	Increase oxygen level. Change one-third of the water, clean filter. Appropriate medications.
Loss of color, spreading beltlike from the middle of the body	Neon disease	Very difficult, with medications. Vitamins as a supporting measure.

OBSERVING BEHAVIOR

If you take a little time to watch the fish in your aquarium, you can observe many interesting behavioral patterns. The information on the following pages will help you to understand the behavior of your fish and how to best respond to it.

Reproductive Behavior

In courtship, mating, spawning, and brood care, there are many interesting patterns of behavior to observe. Many fish change their color before or during courtship; many, like the Siamese Fighting Fish, put on an extraordinary courtship display.

Siamese Fighting Fish (*Betta splendens*): When the male flares his gill covers, he is not always preparing and looking for a fight. In the wild, fighting is the exception, it rarely occurs. In the muddy rice paddies of Asia, the rival can barely be detected a few inches away. In a clean aquarium, the Fighting Fish sees rivals in all long-finned tank mates and must drive them off. But before doing so, he expands his gills and spreads his splendid fins in order to impress his female. Simultaneously, this fish with his martial arts name is an extremely loving father. He builds his bubble nest by himself at the water surface and then looks for a female and entices

A pair of Paradise Fish, the male on the left, at the nest before spawning.

her to the nest. There he embraces the female and fertilizes the eggs. When they sink to the bottom, he gathers them and blows them, enveloped in slime, into the nest. Once the fry have hatched, if one of them should fall out of the nest, he catches it and puts it back, for the young cannot swim at first. After a while, they float out of the nest. Since the father has eaten nothing during the whole time, he is often so exhausted that he never recovers.

Swordtails (*Xiphophorus helleri*): This fish also displays very interesting and unusual courtship behavior. The male, while swimming backward with his sword (caudal fin) bent at a 90 degree angle, circles the female at breathtaking speed. His movements are fascinating. To this day researchers have not determined how the male, with his flexed caudal fin, can swim backward so quickly. Suddenly, the male stops near the female and fertilizes her. The sperm packet that is transferred is sufficient for several successful broods. After the eggs rupture, the fry of Live-bearing Swordtails sink to the bottom and need about four to six hours before they can swim.

INTERPRETER

You can make many interesting observations if you know how to interpret the behavior of your aquarium fish correctly.

 My aquarium fish displays this behavior.

 What does my fish mean by it?

 This is how I correctly respond to its behavior!

Male Gourami touches the female with his pectoral fins.

He is ready to mate.

Avoid any commotion around the aquarium.

Gourami blows foam onto the water surface.

The male is building a nest.

Avoid any commotion around the aquarium.

Fry gather around the male.

The male is guarding them.

The animals need enough hiding places in the aquarium.

Golden Angelfish are eating eggs.

They are removing unfertilized eggs from the spawn.

Do not panic; they are eating only the unfertilized eggs.

All the fish are swimming to the food tablet offered.

The food is being accepted.

You can continue to use the same food.

Male Fighting Fish expands his gills.

He wants to impress his female.

The animals need enough space to avoid territorial battles.

Male Fighting Fish embraces the female.

The female is spawning.

Avoid any commotion around the aquarium.

Fish (here two male Emperor Tetras) suddenly change their color.

This—along with bumping their bodies and fins against each other as they swim side by side— is typical courtship behavior.

No cause for alarm, this is not a pathological change.

Red Swordtails—the lower fish clearly displays the long caudal fin for which it is named.

Schooling Behavior

Even in the aquarium, a number of fish species display definite schooling behavior. Barbs, Characins, and many Catfish are typical examples. The school offers protection from hungry enemies. A predator finds picking one particular fish out of a school to be almost impossible. The weak fish, in particular, cannot keep up with the school and so fall prey to the hunters.

The fry of these species, for example the Kribensis (*Pelvicachromis pulcher*), which seeks protection in a cave when breeding, also keep together as a school. The colorful female, with her fiery red flank blotch, guards the fry in the cave into which the male has guided her. While swimming on his side, the male displays the ovoid spot on his caudal fin. The eggs are attached to the roof of the cave. A little while after hatching, the school of fry is led out by both parents to eat. Initially, the farther away the parents move while defending the school, the closer the fry huddle together in a depression. They are then scarcely visible. The school offers the best protection, even for fry.

Territoriality

Some fish like a specific area for themselves in the aquarium. Territories can be places for

*Cardinal Tetras are schooling fish
that are very effective because of their
brilliant colors.*

breeding and rearing young, as with the Cichlids. Territories can also be spawning territories,
as with some Barbs and Characins.

In order to get in the mood, the Emperor
Tetra (*Nematobrycon palmeri*) needs a spawning territory with lots of feathery Java Moss or
similar plants. There you can observe how two
male Emperor Tetras (recognized by the elongated middle fin rays) swim alongside each

other, suddenly trembling with excitement.
Their bodies seem to touch, they strike each
other with their caudal fins. Their colors are
much more intense than usual. The females lay
a few eggs at a time over an extended period
(about 48 hours). The males fertilize these eggs
as they are laid. Since not many fry hatch at
the same time, small Emperor Tetras of all sizes
are gathered together in the moss. Enough
microscopic food is available in the dense cover
so that even in a community aquarium, a few
fry can always reach maturity. The selected
spawning territory is thus the best place for
the young to grow into adults.

The Variable Platy is closely related to the Swordtail.

Addresses

Federation of American Aquarium Societies
Att: Sally Van Camp
923 Wadsworth Street
Syracuse, NY 13208

Aqualand Aquatic Society
PO Box 1345
Bristol, CT 06010-1345

American Aquarist Society, Inc.
Box 100
3901 Hatch Boulevard
Sheffield, AL 35660
205-386-7687

Atlantis Tropical
830 East Monona Drive
Phoenix, AZ 85024

Green Water Aquarist Society
PO Box 62
Worth, IL 60482
pwp.stametinc.com

Useful Books

Schliewen, Ulrich: *Aquarium Fish.* Barron's
    Educational Series, Inc., Hauppauge, New
    York. 1992.
Stadelmann, P.: *The Natural Aquarium Handbook.*
    Barron's Educational Series, Inc., Hauppauge,
    New York. 2000.
Riehl, R. and Baensch, H. A.: *Aquarium Atlas*
    (3 volumes). Microcosm, Ltd., Shelburne, VT.
    1997.
Carrington, N.: *A Fishkeeper's Guide to a Healthy
    Aquarium.* Tetra Press, Morris Plains, NJ. 1990.

Periodicals

The Rainbow Times, Rainbowfish Study Group,
    Cookville, TN
Tropical Fish Hobbyist, T.F.H. Publications, Inc.,
    Neptune City, NJ
Aquarium Fish magazine, Boulder, CO

The Photographs

Kahl: Inside front cover, 12 top left, bottom left, 13 bottom right, 14, 16, 18 top left, bottom left, top right, bottom right, 19 top left, bottom right, 24, 27, 29, 32, 39, 40, 41, 46, 52, 54, 55, 56 top right, bottom right, 57 top right, bottom right, 59, 61;

Linke: pages 4–5, 9, 12 bottom right, 13 center left, 17, 19 top right, 36, 38, 56 top left, bottom left, 57 center right;

Lucas: pages 2–3, 57 top left;

Nieuwenhuizen: pages 8, 12 top right, 13 top left, bottom left, top right, center right, 19 bottom left, 20, 37, 42–43, 51, 57 bottom left, 58, 64–inside back cover;

Peither: Front cover (large photo), 10, 11, 18 center right, 25, 28, 50;

Schmida: pages 6–7, 19 center right;

Werner: Front cover (small photo), back cover.

Cover Photos

Front cover: The lively Platy depicted here thrive on algae and group interaction.

Back cover: Cichlid.

Page 1: Two Tiger Barbs (*Puntius tetrazona*).

Pages 2–3: The Upside-down Catfish is interesting to observe because of its unusual way of swimming.

Pages 4–5: Kribensis (*Pelvicachromis pulcher*) with fry.

Pages 6–7: Iridescent colors distinguish the Rainbowfish; here *Melanotaenia trifasciata*.

Electric devices for aquarium maintenance are described in this book. It is imperative that you follow the advice on page 27.

Before purchasing a large aquarium, test the load-bearing capacity of the floor in your home at the intended site. Water damage caused by breakage of the glass, overflowing, or leaking of the tank cannot always be avoided. Therefore, be sure to take out insurance.

Be careful that children do not eat aquarium plants. Serious illness can result. Keep fish medications out of the reach of children. You can injure yourself on the spines of some fish species. Since these stab wounds can cause allergic reactions, you must go to a doctor at once.

About the Author

Peter Stadelmann is a pet dealer as well as a trainer and examiner for retail dealers in the pet trade with the Nuremberg Chamber of Commerce. He has already written several books about aquariums and garden ponds for GU Naturbuch.

About the Artist

György Jankovics is a trained graphic artist. He studied at the art academies of Budapest and Hamburg. He draws animal and plant subjects for a number of respected publishing houses. He has also illustrated many books for GU Naturbuch-Verlag.

English language edition © Copyright 2000 by Barron's Educational Series, Inc.
Translated from the German by Mary Lynch.
©Copyright 1998 by Grafe und Unzer Verlag GmbH, Munich, Germany

Original German title is *Das Aquarium*

All inquiries should be addressed to:
Barron's Educational Series, Inc.
250 Wireless Boulevard
Hauppauge, NY 11788
http://www.barronseduc.com
ISBN-13: 978-0-7641-1179-2
ISBN-10: 0-7641-1179-5
Library of Congress Catalog Card No. 99-047358

Library of Congress Cataloging-in-Publication Data
Stadelmann, Peter.
  [Aquarium. English.]
  Setting up an aquarium / Peter Stadelmann ; with illustrations by György Jankovics.
      p. cm.
  "Original German title is Das aquarium"—T.p. verso.
  Includes bibliographical references.
  ISBN 0-7641-1179-5
  1. Aquariums. 2. Aquarium fishes. I. Title.
SF457.S59713   2000
639.34—dc21   99-047358

Printed in China
19 18 17 16 15 14 13 12 11

1 I would like to buy an aquarium. What size is right for me?

Children can best observe and care for a 24-inch (60-cm) aquarium by themselves; a good size for adult is 30 to 40 inches (80 to 100 cm) long.

2 Do I need permission from the landlord for an aquarium?

Policies vary, but it's always a good idea to check with your landlord before investing in a tank.

3 What is the best stand for my aquarium?

The base should be made especially for the aquarium. If an adult sits on it and nothing wobbles, the base wil bear the weight of a small tank.

4 Will the lights and running pumps be disturbing?

Even from 1 yard (1 m) away, practically nothing can b· heard from an aquarium. The light is turned off at nigh

5 Can I actually develop a relationship with the fish?

After a while, many fish will come to recognize their caretaker by the rhythm of his or her steps and perhaps even eat from his or her hand.